Cursive Handwriting Workbook for Young Teens

Practice Workbook with Fun Facts about Dinosaurs that Build Knowledge in a Young Teenager

Cursive Handwriting Workbook for Young Teens: Practice Workbook with Fun Facts about Dinosaurs that Build Knowledge in a Young Teenager
Copyright © 2020 by Ellie Roberts

Introduction to Cursive Handwriting

The goal of this workbook is to help you develop or improve your handwriting skills. It is designed for beginners and intermediates since it mostly focuses on the cursive writing of entire words and sentences.

This book does, however, contain a short practice section for each letter. This overview includes recommendations on how each letter should be written. The rest of the workbook contains interesting facts about the Mesozoic Era, dinosaurs, and paleontology.

Each exercise is composed of two parts. The first part contains words extracted from the sentence, written with a traceable cursive font. The second part contains a worksheet designed for the entire sentence to be rewritten multiple times if possible.

Learning the skill of cursive handwriting has numerous benefits. By pairing these benefits with the knowledge gained from the dinosaur facts, the value you get from completing each exercise increases exponentially.

Each fact is short and easy to remember. The acquired knowledge can help you start interesting conversations with friends and family.

Happy Practicing!

Cursive uppercase letters

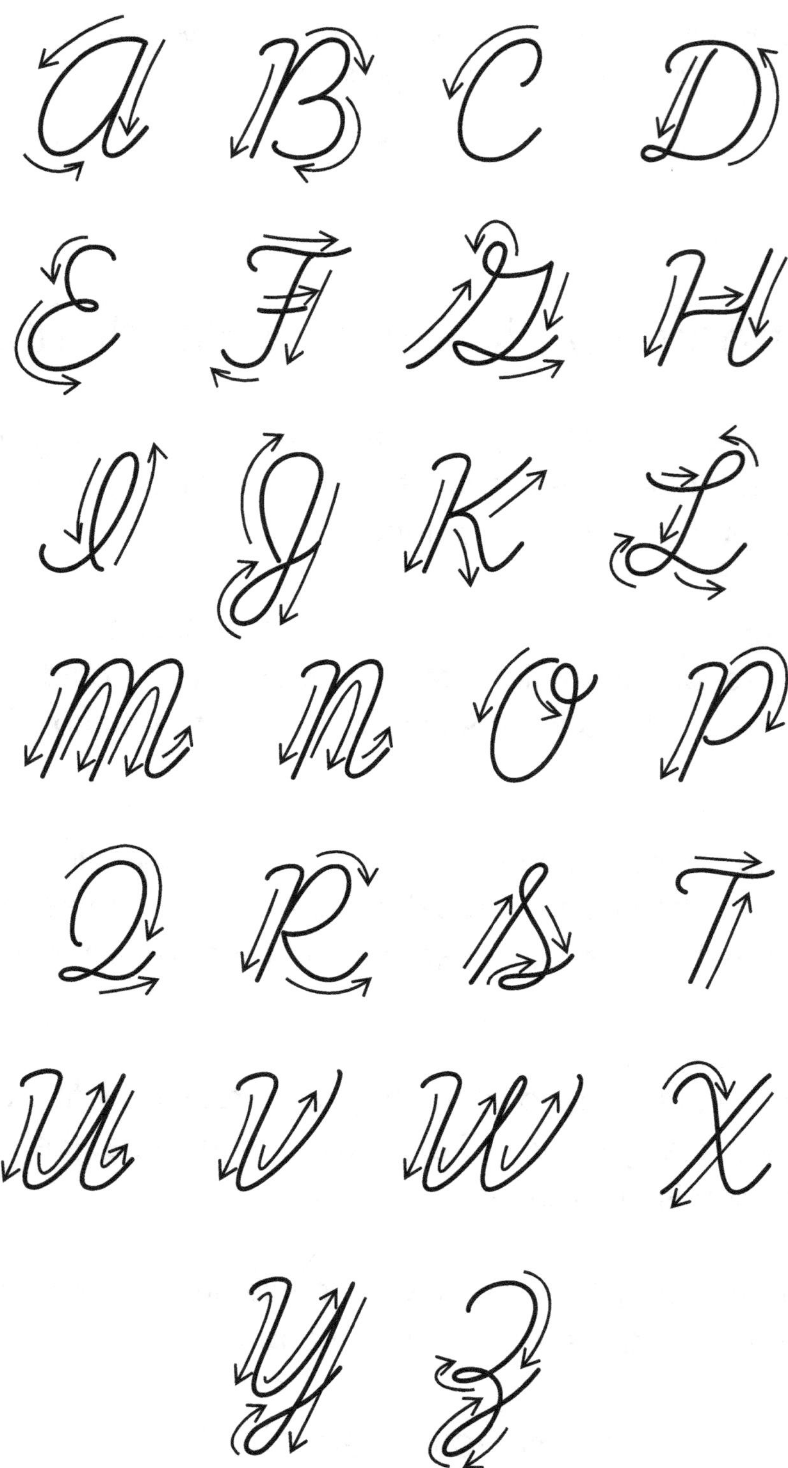

Cursive lowercase letters

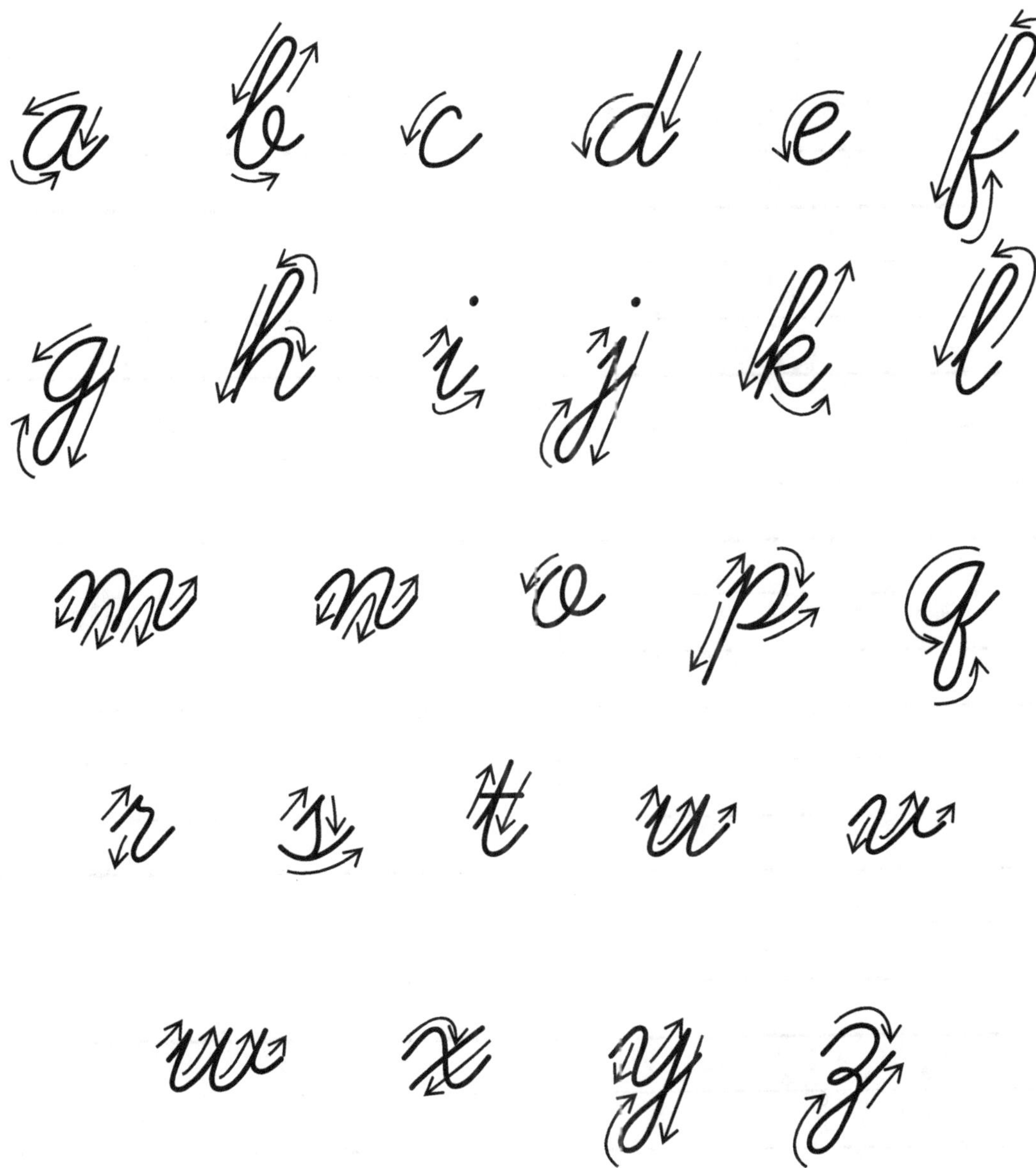

<u>Cursive letter practice</u>

e

F

f

G

g

H

h

I

i

J

t

U

u

V

v

W

w

X

x

Y

Fact #1:

Humans have been on Earth for 2.5 million years. Dinosaurs, however, roamed our planet for approximately 160 million years.

Humans

Earth

Dinosaurs

million

Copy the entire previous quote below while using your best handwriting.

Fact #2:

The Velociraptor's name means "speedy thief." This dinosaur's name is commonly shortened to "raptor."

Velociraptor

speedy

thief

name

Copy the entire previous quote below while using your best handwriting.

The Tyrannosaurus rex had a bite more than twice as powerful as that of a lion.

rex

bite

powerful

lion

Copy the entire previous quote below while using your best handwriting.

Because of their size, some of the largest herbivorous dinosaurs had to eat as much as one ton of food per day.

Because

herbivorous

eat

food

Copy the entire previous quote below while using your best handwriting.

Fact #5:

According to scientists, most dinosaurs were human-sized or smaller. Larger bones are found more frequently because they were more easily fossilized.

According

scientists

bones

fossilized

Copy the entire previous quote below while using your best handwriting.

Fact #6:

Meat-eating dinosaurs had sharp, hooked claws
on their toes and are called "theropods."

sharp

hooked

claws

toes

Copy the entire previous quote below while using your best handwriting.

Fact #7:
Herbivorous dinosaurs are commonly
characterized by their blunt hooves or toenails.

commonly

blunt

hooves

toenails

Copy the entire previous quote below while using your best handwriting.

Fact #8:
Some dinosaurs had tails that exceeded 45 feet (14 meters) in length. These tails were there to help them keep their balance while running.

tails

exceeded

balance

running

Copy the entire previous quote below while using your best handwriting.

Fact #9:

The Eoraptor is the earliest named dinosaur found so far. Its name means "dawn stealer."

Eoraptor

earliest

named

dinosaur

Copy the entire previous quote below while using your best handwriting.

Dinosaurs are divided into two groups based on the structure of their hip bones. Lizard-hipped dinosaurs had bones pointing forward, whereas bird-hipped dinosaurs had bones pointing backwards.

divided

groups

structure

hip

Copy the entire previous quote below while using your best handwriting.

Fact #11:

The term "dinosaur," meaning "terrible lizard," was first coined by Richard Owen in the year 1842.

terrible

lizard

first

coined

Copy the entire previous quote below while using your best handwriting.

Fact #12:

Some of the most famous dinosaurs, like the Brachiosaurus and the Triceratops, only appeared later during the Jurassic and Cretaceous periods.

Triceratops

Jurassic

Cretaceous

periods

Copy the entire previous quote below while using your best handwriting.

Fact #13:

The first dinosaurs were small and lightweight, and are believed to have appeared 230 million years ago during the Triassic period.

small

lightweight

appeared

Triassic

Copy the entire previous quote below while using your best handwriting.

Fact #14:

The Micropachycephalosaurus is the dinosaur with the longest name. Its name translates to "small thick-headed lizard."

longest

name

translates

small

Copy the entire previous quote below while using your best handwriting.

Fact #15:

Scientists believe that the average lifespan of a dinosaur was around 30-40 years.

average

lifespan

around

years

Copy the entire previous quote below while using your best handwriting.

Fact #16:

It's been estimated that more than 1,000 different species of non-avian dinosaurs existed on our planet.

estimated

different

non-avian

existed

Copy the entire previous quote below while using your best handwriting.

Fact #17:

The Cretaceous-Tertiary extinction event (or the K-T event) refers to the mass extinction of the dinosaurs that occurred 65.5 million years ago.

extinction

event

refers

mass

Fact #18:

The first complete Plesiosaurus was discovered by Mary Anning (1799-1847), who was one of the most famous fossil hunters of her time.

complete

Plesiosaurus

Mary

Anning

Copy the entire previous quote below while using your best handwriting.

Fact #19:

Scientists believe that plant-eating dinosaurs might have been cold-blooded, because they were not very active. Meanwhile, meat-eaters were probably warm-blooded.

Scientists

might

active

probably

Copy the entire previous quote below while using your best handwriting.

Fact #20:

The first dinosaur nest was discovered in the Gobi Desert in Mongolia in the year 1923 by Explorer Roy Chapman Andrews and his crew.

Gobi

Desert

Mongolia

crew

Copy the entire previous quote below while using your best handwriting.

Fact #21:
Some dinosaur eggs were as large as modern-day basketballs.

Some

eggs

large

basketballs

Copy the entire previous quote below while using your best handwriting.

The Triceratops, meaning "three-horned face," had a skull that could grow up to 6 and a half feet (2 m) in length and a bony shield over its neck.

skull

bony

shield

neck

Copy the entire previous quote below while using your best handwriting.

Fact #23:

A majority of the dinosaurs that existed on our planet were plant-eaters.

majority

existed

planet

were

Copy the entire previous quote below while using your best handwriting.

Fact #24:

The Liopleurodon was the biggest aquatic reptile
and measured approximately 50 feet (15 meters).

biggest

aquatic

reptile

measured

Copy the entire previous quote below while using your best handwriting.

Fact #25:

Most carnivorous dinosaurs had low-density bones filled with pockets of air. This made them lighter and allowed them to be more agile while hunting.

carnivorous

pockets

agile

hunting

Copy the entire previous quote below while using your best handwriting.

$$Fact\ \#26:$$

The smartest type of dinosaurs were most likely
small carnivores.

smartest

type

likely

small

Copy the entire previous quote below while using your best handwriting.

Fact #27:

Most plant-eating dinosaurs were able to watch for danger while eating because they had eyes on either side of their head.

watch

danger

eyes

head

Copy the entire previous quote below while using your best handwriting.

Fact #28:
Most adult dinosaurs had brains smaller than
that of a newborn human baby.

adult

dinosaurs

brains

newborn

Copy the entire previous quote below while using your best handwriting.

In order to better carry their heavy bodies, most herbivore dinosaurs had to walk on four feet. However, some of these plant-eaters were able to balance on two feet for a short time.

carry

four

feet

balance

Copy the entire previous quote below while using your best handwriting.

Most carnivorous dinosaurs walked on two feet. This made them a lot faster while running and enabled them to grab their prey with their free hands.

walked

faster

enabled

prey

Copy the entire previous quote below while using your best handwriting.

Fact #31:
Scientists believe that dinosaurs may have shed their skin when they grew.

may

shed

skin

grew

Copy the entire previous quote below while using your best handwriting.

Fact #32:

The T-rex ate up to 22 tons of meat a year.
Because this dinosaur couldn't chew, it swallowed
its food in large chunks.

tons

year

swallowed

chunks

Copy the entire previous quote below while using your best handwriting.

Fact #33:

The Tyrannosaurus rex had jagged teeth that were 6 to 12 inches (15 - 30 cm) long.

jagged

teeth

inches

long

Copy the entire previous quote below while using your best handwriting.

Fact #34 :

The Deinosuchus translates to "terrible crocodile." This was a huge prehistoric crocodile that weighed eight times as much as today's crocodile.

translates

crocodile

prehistoric

eight

Copy the entire previous quote below while using your best handwriting.

Fact #35:

Scientists believe that plant-eating dinosaurs may have contributed to Mesozoic global warming by passing gas.

contributed

Mesozoic

global

warming

Copy the entire previous quote below while using your best handwriting.

Fact #36:

The tallest dinosaurs that ever lived were part of the Sauropod group.

tallest

lived

Sauropod

group

Copy the entire previous quote below while using your best handwriting.

Fact #37:

Some researchers believe that the Tyrannosaurus rex
was able to run as fast as 18 mph
(28 km/h).

researchers

believe

fast

run

Copy the entire previous quote below while using your best handwriting.

All dinosaurs reproduced by laying eggs. Scientists estimate that trillions of dinosaur eggs were laid during the Mesozoic Era.

laying

estimate

trillions

Mesozoic

Copy the entire previous quote below while using your best handwriting.

Fact #39:

The biggest carnivorous dinosaur was the Spinosaurus. It could grow up to 59 feet (18 meters) in length.

biggest

Spinosaurus

grow

length

Copy the entire previous quote below while using your best handwriting.

Fact #40:
The toothiest of all dinosaurs was the Hadrosaur.
It had over 1,000 cheek teeth.

toothiest

Hadrosaur

over

cheek

Copy the entire previous quote below while using your best handwriting.

Fact #41:

The largest flying reptile was the Quetzalcoatlus.
Its wingspan could reach up to 39 feet (12 m).

largest

flying

reptile

wingspan

Copy the entire previous quote below while using your best handwriting.

Fact #42:

The Therizinosaurus had claws that could grow up to 3 feet (1 meter) in length. The name of this dinosaur translates to "reaping lizard."

claws

grow

meter

dinosaur

Copy the entire previous quote below while using your best handwriting.

Fact #43:

So far, the smallest dinosaur egg ever discovered
is about 0.7 inches (18 millimeters) long.

far

smallest

ever

discovered

Copy the entire previous quote below while using your best handwriting.

Fact #44 :

The smartest dinosaur is believed to have been the Troodon. This dinosaur had a brain the size of that of a modern bird.

smartest

Troodon

modern

bird

Copy the entire previous quote below while using your best handwriting.

Fact #45:

By looking at the distances between fossilized footprints, scientists are able to estimate how fast a dinosaur used to walk.

distances

footprints

estimate

walk

Copy the entire previous quote below while using your best handwriting.